The New Orleans Bartender

A Guide to
Fabulous Drinks in the Big Easy

Designed & Illustrated
by
Sean Koskela

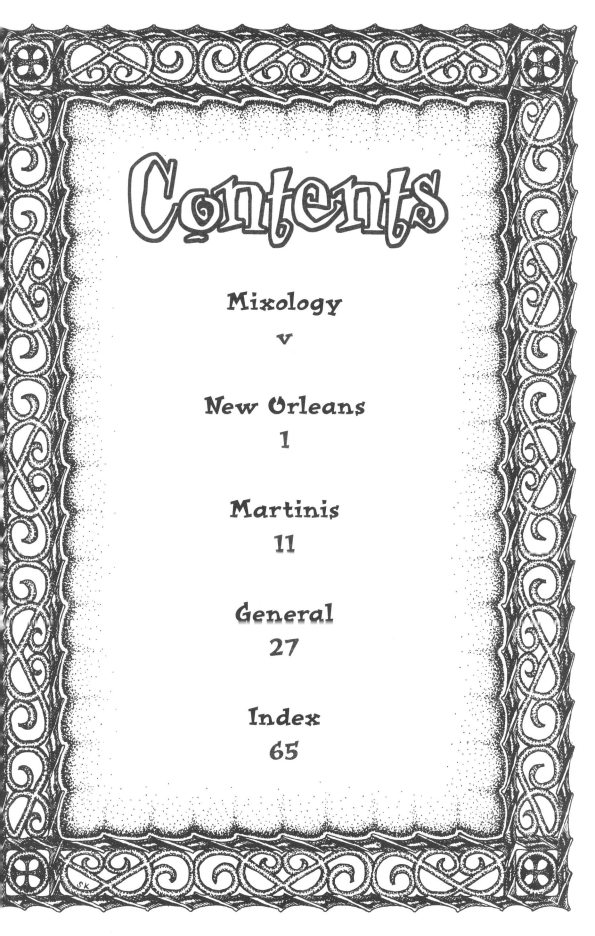

Contents

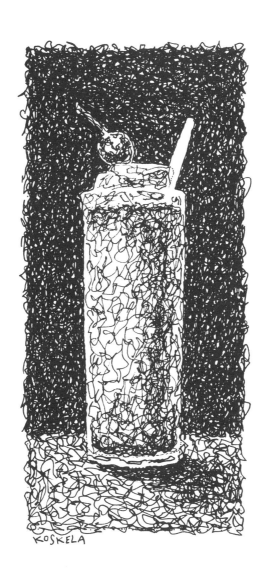

KOSKELA

Mixology

The ingredients we select for mixing drinks are essential in determining our degree of success. For example, many fruit-flavored liqueurs are often used only sparingly to enhance a cocktail's flavor or appearance. Brandies, on the other hand, which are distilled from fermented fruit will often represent the predominant ingredient in a cocktail.

Although their uses may be varied each of the components should be purposely used to produce a delightful mixture. The following ingredients are among those listed in the recipes found in this book.

Absinthe: A somewhat bitter extract from wormwood now illegal in the United States. In earlier days it was considered habit-forming and directly responsible for causing insanity. Substitutes like Pernod and Herbsaint are commonly used in the absinthe-type drinks popular in New Orleans.

Bitters: Usually made from varying combinations and proportions of water, spices, herbs, roots, flowers, fruits, alcohol and coloring. *Peychaud* and *Angostura* bitters are both listed among the recipes.

Blackberry (or any fruit flavored) Liqueur: Predominantly a mixture of blackberries (or other fruit) and brandy with an occasional complement of red wine.

Chambord: A French liqueur with an intense flavor of black raspberries, fruits, herbs and honey. It has a deep ruby red color.

Chaser: A mixer that is tossed down the gullet after one has drunk a straight shot of whiskey or other spirit instead of being combined with a spirit in a glass. The Boilermaker originally was "a shot and a beer", meaning a shot glass of whiskey followed by a beer chaser.

Cocktail: A combination of spirits and flavorings, sweeteners, and garnishes of various kinds intended to be consumed before dining. The usual cocktail consists of a base such as gin, whiskey, rum, brandy, vodka or table wine.

Coco Lopez: The base ingredient of this liqueur is extracted from the coconut.

Cointreau: A liqueur that is a blend of sweet and bitter orange peels.

Collins: Basically a sour in a tall glass with club soda or seltzer water. The famous Tom Collins made with gin has been extended to include everything from applejack (a Jack Collins) to Irish Whiskey (Mike Collins).

Cooler: True coolers are made with ginger ale, club soda, or other carbonated beverage, and the rind of a lemon or orange, cut in a continuous spiral, with one end hooked over the rim of the glass. All coolers are served in tall glasses such as a Collins glass.

Crème de Cacao: A cocoa or chocolate flavored liqueur with a sweet taste and heavy syrup base.

Crème de Menthe: A mint-flavored liqueur with a medium sweetness and distinctive mint aroma.

Curaçao: This orange-based liqueur is extracted from fruit grown on the island of Curaçao. Available in colors by introducing food coloring to the contents.

Dubonnet: French wine based aperitif; Dubonnet blanc, a white wine based spirit; Dubonnet blonde, a dry spirit.

Eggnog: A traditional Christmas holiday bowl containing a combination of eggs, sugar, cream, and brandy, rum or bourbon served cold in cups. A hot drink based on the same ingredients is called a Tom & Jerry.

Fizz: There are many fine old recipes for Fizzes, which are products of the old siphon bottle that "fizzed" the drink with a stream of bubbles. The Gin Fizz is typical and similar to the Tom Collins. Other famous Fizzes are the Ramos Gin Fizz and the Slow Gin Fizz.

Floating: The purpose of floating is to keep each of the ingredients in a drink in separate layers from others. This also refers to layering. The easiest way to float one liquor on top of another is to use a small spoon and slowly trickle the ingredient over the last layer.

Frappé: Anything served with finely crushed ice.

Grand Marnier: A superior imported orange liqueur with a Cognac base.

Grenadine: Customarily non-alcoholic, this red syrup is subtly flavored with pomegranate juice and used generally for color.

Green Chartreuse: A colorful liqueur with a full-bodied aroma. Comprised of an assortment of herbs and spices, this formula is still a well-kept secret.

Grog: Originally a mixture of rum and water that was issued to sailors in the Royal Navy and later improved with the addition of lime juice and sugar. Now a Grog can be most any kind of drink. It is usually made with a rum base, fruit and various sweeteners and served either hot or cold in a large mug or glass.

Highball: Any spirit served with ice and club soda in a medium to tall glass. Other carbonated beverages may be used, but if other ingredients are added, it is no longer a highball.

Julep: A venerable drink made of Kentucky bourbon, sugar, mint leaves, and plenty of crushed ice. A true southern classic.

Maraschino: A cherry-flavored liqueur used for coloring and or adding a distinctive sweet taste. Maraschino cherries are often used as garnish.

Mist: A glass is packed with crushed ice to which spirits are added. No mix is added.

Mixing: When using a cocktail shaker, the ice should always be put into the shaker first, the liquor last. This is to ensure that all ingredients are properly chilled by the ice when they are poured over the ice. Adding the liquor last reduces the change of dilution.

Muddle: Muddle is a mashing technique for combining items such as herbs, sugar, fruit in the bottom of a glass before adding other ingredients.

On-the-Rocks: Any wine or spirit poured over ice cubes, usually in an Old Fashioned glass.

Orange-flower Water: A lightly flavored non-alcoholic extract which originated in France.

Orgeat Syrup: An almond based non-alcoholic syrup.

Peppar: A vodka with an fiery, complex taste of chili peppers.

Pisang Ambon: An emerald green exotic specialty from Indonesia that gets its flavor from tropical fruits.

Rickey: A drink made with gin or other spirit, lime juice, and club soda. It is usually served with ice in a small highball or Rickey glass, with or without sweetening. Named for Colonel Joe Rickey, an old-time Washington lobbyist.

Sambuca: An Italian licorice flavored liqueur.

Schnapps: A generic name for a flavorful alcoholic beverage made from grain or potato spirits and flavored with various fruits or herbs. They can range from sweet liqueur to a dry one such as infused vodka.

Shaking: Drinks that contain ingredients such as cream, fruit juices and eggs should be shaken vigorously to ensure that all ingredients have been mixed well.

Shooter: A straight shot of whiskey or other kind of spirit taken in a single gulp without any accompaniment.

Simple Syrup: Sugar syrup can be made from equal parts of water and sugar that is heated until sugar dissolves and then cooled.

Sling: A tall drink made with lemon juice, sugar, and spirits, usually served cold with club soda. The most famous sling is the Singapore Sling.

Sloe Gin: A liqueur flavored with sloe, a wild black plum.

Smash: A short julep made with spirits, sugar, and mint, usually served in an Old Fashioned glass.

Sour: A short drink made of lemon or lime juice, sugar and spirits. The Whiskey Sour is the classic sour, but it may be made with vodka, gin, rum, or brandy. Often various liqueurs such as apricot or peach liqueur is added.

Stirring: A drink that is stirred instead of shaken will retain its clarity and be free of chips. Drinks like a Martini should always be stirred, not shaken. Drinks containing carbonated beverages should also be stirred, not shaken.

Sweet/Sour Mix: Equal parts of lemon juice and simple syrup.

Toddy: Usually a hot drink made with spirits, sugar, spices and lemon peel mixed with hot water and served in a tall glass. It can also be served cold with ice.

Setting Up the Bar!

❖ Because people are drinking less alcohol now, you'll likely need more wine, bottled water and soft drinks than you did in years past.

❖ Stick with the basics in liquor — Whiskey, scotch, gin, vodka, tequila, rum and vermouth for cocktails. Wine and beer to drink alone.

❖ Buy plenty of mixers — Tonic water, carbonated water, lemon-lime carbonated beverage, ginger ale.

❖ Have plenty of garnishes available — Maraschino cherries, olives, lemon and lime peels and lemon and lime wedges.

❖ Allow about a pound of ice cubes per person.

❖ You will need the following glasses: 10 or 12 ounce all purpose glasses (for highballs and Collins drinks), 9-10 ounce stemmed wineglasses, Old-Fashioned glasses, Martini glasses for cocktails and cordials, Brandy snifters are good additions to the glass collection.

❖ Equipment necessary for a bar would be a bottle opener, corkscrew, ice crusher, shaker, blender, cocktail napkins, towels and wastebasket.

Tips

❖ 1/2 ounce of liquor is equal to 1 count if you are using a pourer on your bottles. If you want 1 1/2 ounce of liquor, count 1001, 1002, 1003 as you are pouring.

❖ A "Shotglass" is usually 1.5 ounces, but sometimes they are 2 ounces with a marker for 1.5 ounces.

❖ To make highballs, fill glass 2/3 full of ice before adding liquor. Always add the liquor before the mix. Do not stir drinks containing carbonated mixers.

❖ To make drinks requiring a shaker, fill shaker 1/2 full of ice (crushed or cubes) before adding liquor.

❖ In drinks that are blended using cream, most often you can substitute vanilla ice cream for the cream.

❖ Always keep fruit juices and carbonated beverages used in mixed drinks in the refrigerator. Vermouth for martinis, etc. should also be kept chilled.

❖ Always use fresh fruit if available for drinks that have these as ingredients.

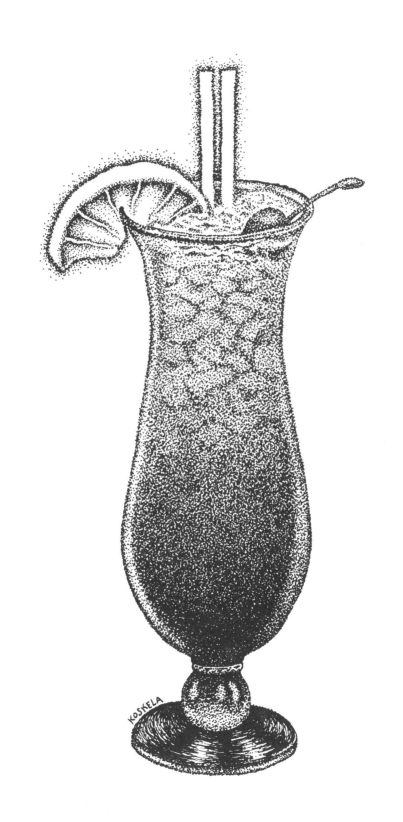

Absolut Ultimate Shooter

1	raw oyster or clam
1	ounce Absolut Peppar
1	teaspoon cocktail sauce
1	lemon wedge

Place oyster or clam in a shot glass with a shot of Absolut Peppar topped with a spoonful of cocktail sauce and a squeeze of lemon. Wow!

Between the Sheets

| 1/2 | ounce each: rum, brandy, Triple Sec, lime juice |

Mix together in shaker with ice. Strain and serve in a rocks or cocktail glass.

KOSKELA

New Orleans

Bloody Mary

1 1/2	ounces vodka
3	ounces tomato juice
1/2	teaspoon lemon juice
1/2	teaspoon Worcestershire sauce
2-3	drops hot pepper sauce
	pepper and salt

Shake with ice and strain into an old-fashioned glass over ice cubes and a wedge of lime.

Cafe Brulot

Dramatic and perfect at the end of a Creole meal.

8	ounces brandy
4	ounces Grand Marnier (or orange-flavored liqueur)
8	teaspoons brown sugar
16	each julienne strips of orange and lemon (about 2 whole)
10	whole cloves
	thin slice of butter
	ground cinnamon
4	cups strong black coffee (New Orleans chicory coffee is great)

In a chafing dish pour the brandy and Grand Marnier. Add the sugar, orange and lemon strips, whole cloves and butter. When the butter begins to melt and the mixture is simmering, light the mixture (best if you ignite some of the mixture in a ladle). Pour ladle that is aflame into rest of mixture. Sprinkle with cinnamon and slowly add the coffee to extinguish the flame. Strain serve in demitasse or brulot cups. Serves 8-10

Grasshopper

1	ounce Green Crème de Menthe
1	ounce White Crème de Cacao
1	ounce cream

Mix all ingredients in a shaker with cracked ice. Strain into a chilled cocktail glass.

Harvey Wallbanger

1 1/2	ounces vodka
4	ounces orange juice
1/2	ounce Galliano

Pour vodka and juice into a glass with several ice cubes. Top with Galliano float.

Hurricane

1	splash Grenadine
2	ounces orange juice
4	ounces pineapple juice
1	ounce dark rum

Stir everything together except Grenadine in a hurricane glass with ice. Add splash of Grenadine.

New Orleans Cocktail

1 1/2   *ounces bourbon*
1/2   *ounce Pernod*
   Dash of each: orange bitter, Angostura Bitters, Anisette,
   sugar syrup to taste
   lemon peel

Mix everything except peel with cracked ice in a shaker. Strain and pour into cocktail glass. Add twist of lemon.

New Orleans

New Orleans Old-Fashioned

1/2	teaspoon sugar syrup
1	dash Angostura Bitters
2	teaspoons club soda
1 1/2	ounces whiskey
1	lemon peel

Combine sugar, bitters and club soda in mixing glass and stir until sugar dissolves. Add the whiskey along with several ice cubes, thoroughly stir. Twist lemon over drink and drop.

New Orleans Salty Dog

5	ounces grapefruit juice
1 1/2	ounces vodka
	coarse salt

Coat the rim of a highball glass with salt. Mix vodka and grapefruit juice in another glass with ice and pour into glass with salted rim.

Pernod Cocktail

1/2	ounce water
4	dashes sugar syrup
4	dashes Angostura Bitters
2	ounces Pernod

Put everything except Pernod in an old-fashioned glass half full of crushed ice. Stir well. Add the Pernod and stir again.

Planter's Punch

1	part dark rum
1/2	part Orgeat syrup
2	parts orange juice
1	part pineapple juice

Combine all ingredients. Serve over ice in a Collins glass. Garnish with lime wedge and maraschino cherry.

Ramos Gin Fizz

2	teaspoons sugar
1	egg white
2	dashes orange flower water
1	dash vanilla extract
1 1/2	teaspoons lemon juice
2	ounces half & half
1	ounce gin

Shake and strain into an old-fashioned glass.

Created by Henry C. Ramos, a renowned bartender in New Orleans at the turn of the century, the Ramos Gin Fizz became so popular that on a busy night, Henry would have as many as 30 shaker boys who would pass ice-cold shakers down the line, each giving it a good buffeting as it passed by.

The Saint Charles

1	juice of lime
2	ounces best quality gin
5	ounces tonic water
4	dashes Peychaud Bitters
1	lime wedge

Fill a highball glass with ice cutes. Add the other ingredients. Rub the lime wedge around rim of glass, then add as a garnish. Stir and serve.

The Sazerac

This classic New Orleans cocktail was invented by Antoine Peychaud in the 1790's. The subtle but complex flavors are like a symphony in the mouth. Sip it slowly and enjoy.

1	teaspoon simple syrup or 1 sugar cube
3	dashes Peychaud Bitters
2	ounces rye whiskey
1/4	teaspoon Pernod or Herbsaint

Chill two old-fashioned glasses with crushed ice. Remove ice from one glass and in it place the syrup or a sugar cube with a little water. Add bitters and crush sugar cube until all sugar is dissolved. Add whiskey and several ice cubes and stir. Empty the second glass of crushed ice, add a generous dash of Herbsaint and coat inside of glass thoroughly. Pour out excess and pour in mixture from first glass. Twist lemon peel over drink but do not put into glass.

Scarlett O'Hara

1 1/2   *ounces Southern Comfort*
1 1/2   *ounce cranberry juice*
1   *ounce lime juice*

Combine all three ingredients in a glass with ice. Stir and enjoy!

Voodoo Sunrise

1   *ounce vodka*
1   *ounce white rum*
1   *ounce Grenadine*
        orange juice

Add the rum and vodka in a tall glass. Tilt the glass and add Grenadine down the inside of the glass. Fill with cold orange juice.

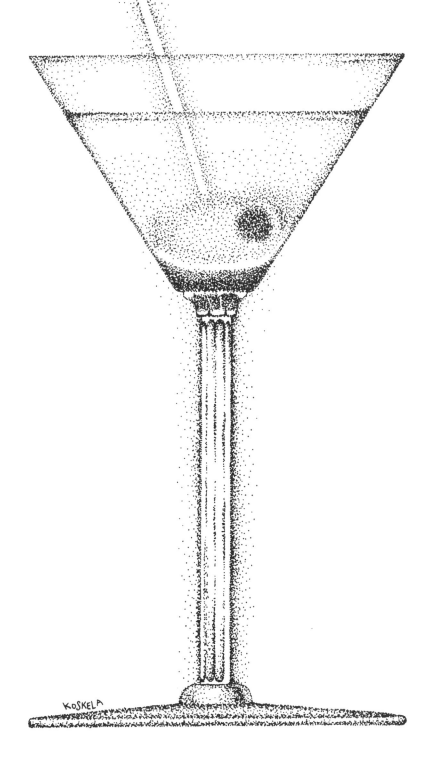

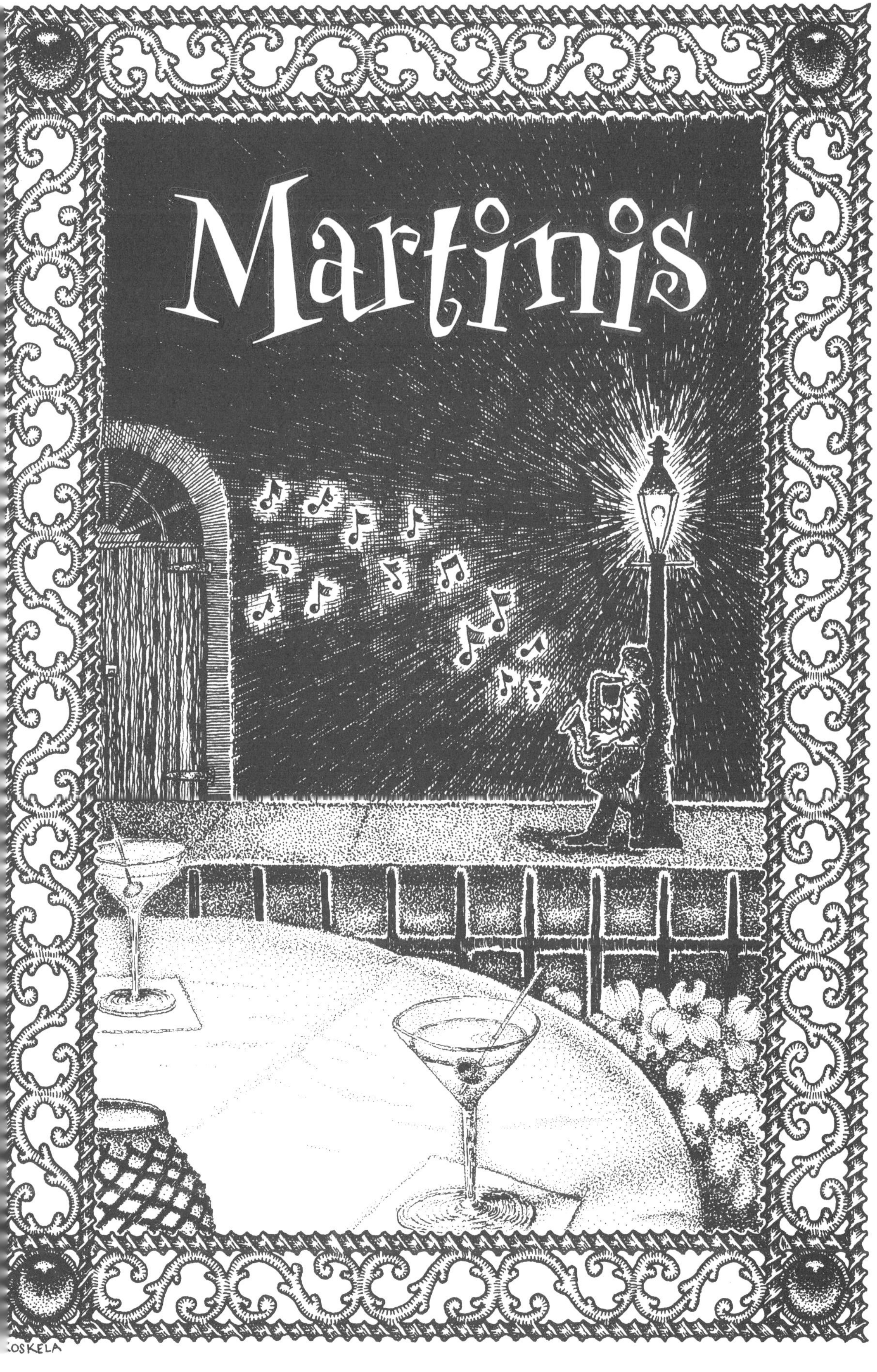
Martinis

The Martini

The Martini is a quintessentially American drink. It has been the perennial king of cocktails for the better part of the 20th century. The origin will probably never be agreed upon. Some say they credit it to a bartender in New York named Martini who first mixed up the concoction in 1912. Others believe it got its name from the dry vermouth commonly used to make the drink, Martini and Rossi. Going back even further, credit could be given to Franciscus de Boe Sylvius. He was a Dutch professor of medicine and he distilled from the oil of juniper berries a product that we now know as gin from the Dutch word for juniper — genever. He intended it to be used as a blood purifier.

KOSKELA

Mixing the Perfect
MARTINI

❖ Gin should always be kept in the freezer. It will not freeze but remain viscous. Vermouth should be kept in refrigerator for maximum flavor. The shaker should be kept in freezer as well.

❖ Ice should be cracked, not crushed and there should be lots of it.

❖ Use precise measurements and freeze shot glass and shaker.

❖ Gin should be poured first through the ice, followed by other ingredients in descending order of amount. (1 oz. before 1/2 oz.)

❖ Stirring is preferable to shaking. Stir about 20 times. If you do shake do so vigorously. and shake only one drink at a time.

❖ Use a good strainer and pour at once into a pre-chilled cocktail glass. Add garnish.

Apple Martini

1   ounce gin
1   ounce Apple Pucker Schnapps
     apple slice for garnish

Pour ingredients over generous amount of ice in a shaker. Shake several times. Strain into a cocktail glass. Garnish with apple slice.

Black and White Martini

3   ounces vanilla-flavored vodka
1   ounce Crème de Cacao
     black and white licorice candies

Pour ingredients over generous amount of ice in a shaker. Shake several times. Strain into a cocktail glass. Garnish with candies.

Bloody Martini

3   ounces Peppar Vodka
3   ounces Citron Vodka
1   ounces Bloody Mary mix

Pour ingredients over generous amount of ice in a shaker. Shake several times. Strain into a cocktail glass rimmed with celery salt. Garnish with a twist of lemon.

Cajun Martini

3   *ounces Peppar Vodka*
      dash of dry vermouth
      olive stuffed with jalapeño pepper

Pour ingredients over generous amount of ice in a shaker. Shake several times. Strain into a cocktail glass. Garnish with olive.

Caribbean Martini

1 1/2 *ounces vanilla-flavored vodka (Stoli)*
3/4   *ounce Malibu Rum*
1   *splash pineapple juice*

Mix all ingredients together in shaker with cracked ice. Strain into cocktail glass.

Chocolate Martini

3   *ounces vodka*
1/2 *ounce chocolate-flavored liqueur (Crème de Cacao)*
      chocolate curl

Pour ingredients over generous amount of ice in a shaker. Shake several times. Strain into a cocktail glass. Garnish with chocolate curl.

Citrus Martini

2	ounces lemon-flavored vodka
1/2	teaspoon orange-flavored liqueur (Grand Marnier)
1/2	teaspoon fresh lime juice
	lemon twist

Pour ingredients over generous amount of ice in a shaker. Shake several times. Strain into a cocktail glass. Garnish with lemon twist.

KOSKELA

Cosmopolitan Martini

3 parts	lemon-flavored vodka
2 parts	orange-flavored liqueur (Grand Marnier)
2 parts	cranberry juice
1	splash lime juice

Pour ingredients over generous amount of ice in a shaker. Shake vigorously. Strain cocktail into a martini glass.

French Martini

1 1/2	ounces Absolut Vodka
1	ounce Chambord Raspberry Liqueur
1	ounce Grand Marnier
1/2	ounce sour Mix (optional)

Pour ingredients over generous amount of ice in a shaker. Shake several times. Strain into a cocktail glass.

Haleakala Martini

1 1/2	ounces Absolut Vodka
1/2	ounce Chambord Raspberry Liqueur
2	ounces pineapple juice

Pour ingredients over generous amount of ice in a shaker. Shake several times. Strain into a cocktail glass.

Iceberg Martini

2 ounces high quality gin
   splash of White Crème de Menthe

Mix in shaker with ice. Strain into cocktail glass. Garnish with mint.

Imperial Martini

2 ounces gin
1/2 ounce dry vermouth
1/2 teaspoon Maraschino Cherry Liqueur
2 dashes Angostura Bitters

Pour ingredients over generous amount of ice in a shaker. Shake several times. Strain into a cocktail glass.

Jamaican Martini

3 ounces gin
1/2 ounce red wine
1 tablespoon dark rum
4 dashes orange bitters

Pour ingredients over generous amount of ice in a shaker. Shake several times. Strain into a cocktail glass.

James Bond Martini

3   ounces gin
1   ounce vodka
1/2   ounce vermouth

Pour ingredients over generous amount of ice in a shaker. Shake several times. Strain into a cocktail glass. Garnish with lime.

KOSKELA

Kahlua Martini

1   *ounce Kahlua*
1   *ounce vodka*
     splash of coffee

Combine over ice in a rocks glass.

Key Lime Martini

2   *ounces vanilla-flavored vodka*
1   *ounce lime juice*
1   *ounce half & half cream*

Pour ingredients over generous amount of ice in a shaker. Shake several times. Strain into a cocktail glass. Serve with a lime twist.

Lemon Drop Martini

3   *ounces Citron Vodka*
1   *teaspoon lemon juice*
1   *teaspoon sugar*

Pour ingredients over generous amount of ice in a shaker. Shake several times. Strain into a cocktail glass. Garnish with a lemon wedge dipped in sugar.

Martini

2 ounces gin
1/2 teaspoon vermouth
olive for garnish

Mix gin and vermouth in a mixing glass with ice. Strain into a chilled cocktail glass. Garnish with the olive.

Mexican Martini

1 1/2 ounces tequila
1/2 ounce Triple Sec

Pour ingredients over generous amount of ice in a shaker. Shake several times. Strain into a cocktail glass. Garnish with a slice of jalapeño pepper.

Mocha Martini

2 1/2 ounces vodka
1/2 ounce Kahlua
1 ounce Crème de Cacao

Mix in shaker with cracked ice. Strain into chilled cocktail glass.

New Orleans Martini

3   ounces vanilla-flavored vodka
1/2   ounce dry vermouth
1/2   ounce Pernod
         dash of Angostura Bitters

Pour ingredients over generous amount of ice in a shaker. Shake several times. Strain into a cocktail glass. Garnish with a sprig of mint.

KOSKELA

Raspberry Martini

1 1/2   ounces raspberry-flavored vodka
3/4   ounce Chambord Raspberry Liqueur
         splash of cranberry juice
         splash of sour mix

Pour ingredients over generous amount of ice in a shaker. Shake several times. Strain into a cocktail glass. Garnish with a fresh raspberry.

The Ricky Martini

2   ounces Puerto Rican rum
1/2   ounce Midori
         splash of dry vermouth
         splash of lime juice

Pour ingredients over generous amount of ice in a shaker. Shake several times. Strain into a cocktail glass. Garnish with a maraschino cherry and lime twist.

Rum Martini

3   ounces light rum
1   ounce dry vermouth
         dash Orange Bitters

Pour ingredients over generous amount of ice in a shaker. Shake several times. Strain into a cocktail glass. Garnish with an almond stuffed olive.

Russian Martini

2	ounces vodka
2	ounces gin
1/2	ounce White Chocolate Liqueur

Pour ingredients over generous amount of ice in a shaker. Shake several times. Strain into a cocktail glass.

Scarlett Martini

1 1/2	ounces Southern Comfort
1 1/2	ounces cranberry juice
1	wedge lime

Mix first two ingredients in shaker with cracked ice. Strain into cocktail glass and garnish with lime.

Spanish Vodka Martini

2 1/2	ounces vodka
1/2	ounce dry sherry

Pour ingredients over generous amount of ice in a shaker. Shake several times. Strain into a cocktail glass. Garnish with a twist of lemon.

Vodka Martini

2   *ounces good quality vodka*
1/2 - 1 teaspoon vermouth
       olive or lemon peel to garnish

Combine vodka and vermouth in mixing glass with generous amount of ice. Stir quickly and strain into glass. Garnish with peel or olive.

General

KOSKELA

Alabama Slammer

1	ounce Amaretto
1	ounce Southern Comfort
1/2	ounce Sloe Gin
1	dash lemon juice

Mix everything except lemon juice in a chilled highball glass. Add lemon juice and stir.

Alexander's Brother

1	ounce gin
1	ounce Crème de Cacao
1	ounce heavy cream

Mix all ingredients in shaker with cracked ice. Mix well. Strain into chilled cocktail glass.

Alexander's Sister

1 1/2	ounces gin
1/2	ounce Green Crème de Menthe
3/4	ounce heavy cream

Mix all ingredients in shaker with cracked ice. Mix well. Strain into chilled cocktail glass.

Amaretto Slinger

1	ounce Amaretto
6	ounces orange juice
1	ounce Sweet & Sour mix
1	ounce vodka

Fill glass 2/3 full of ice. Pour over the above ingredients. Stir gently.

KOSKELA

Apple Brandy Cooler

2	ounces brandy
1	ounce light rum
4	ounces apple juice
1/2	ounce lime juice
1	teaspoon sugar syrup
1	teaspoon Jamaican dark rum
1	slice lime

Mix everything except dark rum and lime) with cracked ice in a shaker. Put in a chilled Collins glass. Float the dark rum on top of drink and use the lime slice as a garnish.

Apple Brandy Highball

2	ounces apple-flavored brandy
	ginger ale

Fill old-fashioned glass 2/3 full of ice. Pour over the brandy and add ginger ale and twist of lemon.

Apricot Brandy Fizz

2	ounces apricot-flavored brandy
3-4	dashes Grenadine
1	orange slice
1	lemon peel
	club soda

Put brandy and Grenadine in a chilled old-fashioned glass with ice cubes. Put in the orange slice and lemon peel, fill with the soda.

B-52

1/2	ounce Kahlua
1/2	ounce Irish Cream Liqueur
1/2	ounce Cointreau

Layer ingredients in a shot glass. Do not stir. Pow!

Bahama Mama

1	dash Amaretto
1	maraschino cherry
1	dash Grenadine
2	ounces pineapple juice
2	ounces dark rum
1/2	teaspoon sugar syrup

Mix everything in a blender except the cherry. Pour over crushed ice and toss in the cherry.

Banshee

1   *ounce White Crème de Cacao*
1   *ounce Crème de Banana*
1   *ounce light cream*

Mix all ingredients in a shaker with ice. Strain into a cocktail glass.

Barracuda

1	ounce Benedictine
1	ounce gin
2	ounces grapefruit juice

Mix everything in a shaker with cracked ice. Strain into a chilled cocktail glass.

Bermuda Highball

3/4	ounce gin
3/4	ounce brandy
3/4	ounce vermouth
	ginger ale

Fill highball glass 2/3 full of ice. Pour the above ingredients over the ice. Fill with ginger ale. Add a lemon twist.

Bird in Paradise

2	ounces gin
2	teaspoons lemon juice
1	teaspoon sugar
1	teaspoon Grenadine
1	egg white
	club soda

Combine all ingredients except club soda in a shaker with ice. Fill with club soda.

Black Russian

1 1/2   *ounces vodka*
3/4   *ounce Kahlua*

Mix both in a shaker with cracked ice. Pour into glass. Add several dashes lemon juice to make Black Magic.

Blizzard

3   *ounces bourbon*
1   *ounce cranberry juice*
1   *tablespoon lemon juice*
2   *tablespoons sugar syrup*

Mix everything in a shaker with generous amount of cracked ice. Shake until frosty and serve in a tall glass.

Blue Hawaii

1   *ounce Blue Curaçao*
3   *ounces crushed ice*
1   *ounce orange juice*
5   *ounces pineapple juice*
1/2   *ounce dark rum*
1/2   *ounce rum*
1   *maraschino cherry*
1   *orange slice*
1   *pineapple chunk*

Pour crushed ice into blender. Add Curaçao, rum, pineapple and orange juice. Blend until smooth. Pour into wine goblet. Use maraschino cherry, orange slice and pineapple chunk for garnish.

Bootlegger

1	ounce whiskey
1	ounce tequila
1	ounce Southern Comfort

Fill old-fashioned glass 2/3 full of ice. Add the above ingredients. Stir.

Brandy Alexander

1 1/2	ounce brandy
1	ounce Crème de Cacao
1	ounce heavy cream

Mix all ingredients in a shaker with cracked ice. Strain into a chilled cocktail glass.

Brandy Fizz

2-3	ounces brandy
1 1/2	ounces lemon juice
1/2	ounce sugar syrup
	club soda to fill glass

Mix everything except soda with cracked ice in a shaker. Pour into a chilled highball glass. Fill with club soda and more ice if necessary.

Brown Cow

1   *ounce Amaretto*
2   *ounces milk*

Mix in shaker with ice. Pour into old-fashioned glass.

Cape Cod Cooler

2   *ounces Sloe Gin*
1   *ounce gin*
5   *ounces cranberry juice*
1/2   *ounce lemon juice*
1/2   *ounce Orgeat Syrup*
1   *lime slice*

Mix everything except lime slice in a shaker with cracked ice. Pour into a chilled Collins glass. Use the lime slice as a garnish.

Champagne Bayou

2   *ounces Gin*
2   *teaspoon sugar syrup*
1   *teaspoon lemon juice*
       champagne

Combine ingredients except champagne in shaker with ice. Pour into Collins glass and fill with champagne.

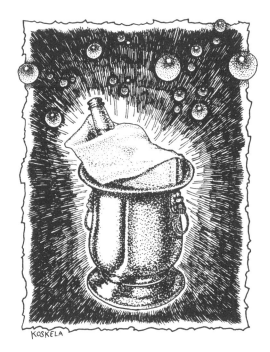

KOSKELA

Champagne Cooler

1   *ounce brandy*
1   *ounce Cointreau*
      champagne to fill glass
2   *mint sprigs*

Pout brandy and cointreau in a chilled wine goblet. Fill with champagne and stir gently. Garnish with mint sprigs

Chelada

12   *ounces beer*
      juice of 1 lemon
      salt to taste

Mix ingredients in a Collins glass with lots of ice. Enjoy!

Cherry Sour

1 1/2 ounce Cherry Marnier
3/4   ounce gin
       juice of 1/2 lemon

Mix everything in a shaker with cracked ice. Strain into a chilled cocktail glass.

Cranberry Cooler

1 1/2 ounces Amaretto
1 1/2 ounces cranberry juice
1 1/2 ounces orange juice

Combine ingredients in shaker with ice. Pour into highball glass.

Cranberry Kamikaze

1   ounce vodka
1   ounce orange-flavored liqueur
1/2   ounce lime juice
1   teaspoon sugar syrup
1/4   cup cranberry juice

Mix all ingredients in a shaker with ice. Pour into a chilled cocktail glass.

Curacao Cooler

1 1/2   ounces Blue Curaçao
1   ounce light rum
5   ounces orange juice
1   ounce lime juice
1   orange peel twist

Mix everything except orange peel with cracked ice in a shaker. Pour into a chilled Collins glass. Twist the peel over the glass and drop it into the glass.

Derby Daiquiri

1 1/2   ounces white rum
1   ounce orange juice
2   teaspoons lime juice
2   teaspoons sugar syrup

Combine all ingredients with 1/2 cup cracked ice in a blender for 20 seconds. Strain and serve in cocktail glass.

Dixie

1   ounce gin
1/2   ounce Pernod
1/2   ounce dry vermouth
1-2   ounces orange juice
3-4   ounces Grenadine

Mix everything with cracked ice in a shaker. Strain into a chilled old-fashioned glass.

Dr. Pepper

6	*ounces beer*
6	*ounces cola*
1	*ounce Amaretto*

Pour beer into a beer mug. Add the cola and drop in the Amaretto.

Dreamsicle

2	*ounces vanilla-flavored schnapps*
2	*ounces lemon-lime soda*
2	*ounces orange juice*

Fill highball glass 2/3 full of ice. Pour over the ingredients. Stir very gently.

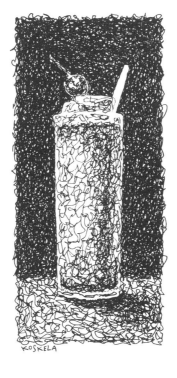

Dubonnet Cocktail

1 1/2   ounces gin
1 1/2   ounces Dubonnet Rouge
1   lemon peel twist

Mix everything except lemon peel with cracked ice in a shaker. Pour into a chilled old-fashioned glass. Twist the peel over the glass and drop it into the drink.

Flying Grasshopper

3/4   ounce Crème de Cacao
3/4   ounce Crème de Menthe
3/4   ounce vodka

Mix all ingredients in a shaker with ice. Strain into a cocktail glass.

Fuzzy Navel

1   ounce vodka
1/2   ounce peach-flavored schnapps
6   ounces orange juice
1   orange slice

Mix everything except orange slice with cracked ice in a shaker. Pour into a chilled Collins glass. Garnish with orange slice.

Georgia Peach

1 1/2 ounces peach-flavored schnapps
3/4 ounce White Crème de Cacao
1 ounce heavy cream
1 peach slice

Mix everything except peach slice with cracked ice in a shaker.
Strain into a chilled cocktail glass. Garnish with peach slice.

Gimlet

2 ounces gin
1/2 ounce lime juice
1 lime peel twist

Mix everything except lime peel with cracked ice in a shaker.
Pour into a chilled old-fashioned glass. Twist the peel over the
glass and drop it into the drink.

Gin and Tonic

2 ounces gin
tonic water to fill glass
1 lime wedge

Pour gin into a chilled Collins glass with several ice cubes. Fill
with tonic water. Squeeze the lime wedge over the glass and drop
it into the drink.

Gin Rickey

1 1/2   *ounces gin*
        club soda to fill glass
        juice of 1/2 lime

Pour gin into a chilled highball glass with some ice cubes. Fill with club soda, add lime juice and stir gently.

Golden Margarita

2	ounces tequila
1	ounce Curaçao
3/4	ounce lime juice

Mix ingredients with cracked ice in a shaker. Rub lemon around rim of cocktail glass, dip in salt. Strain ingredients into glass.

Grand Marnier Margarita

1	ounce tequila
1	ounce Grand Marnier
1	ounce lime juice
	sugar to taste

Wet the rim of a rocks glass with lime juice and dip into salt. Fill a tall shaker with ice. Add tequila, Grand Marnier and lime juice.

High Roller

1 1/2	ounces vodka
3/4	ounce Grand Marnier
4	ounces orange juice
1	teaspoon Grenadine

Mix with ice in shaker. Pour into Collins glass. Garnish with twist of orange peel.

Highland Fling

1 1/2   ounces scotch
3   ounces milk
1   teaspoon sugar syrup
        nutmeg

Mix everything except nutmeg with cracked ice in a shaker. Pour into a chilled old-fashioned glass. Sprinkle with nutmeg.

Irish Cooler

3   ounces whiskey
        club soda

Fill a Collins glass 2/3 full of ice. Pour the whiskey over the ice and fill with club soda. Add a lemon twist.

Irish Mounty

1 1/2   Canadian Whiskey
1   ounce Irish Mist
1/2   ounce heavy cream
        grated nutmeg

Mix everything except nutmeg with cracked ice in a shaker. Strain into a chilled cocktail glass. Sprinkle nutmeg on top.

Jamaica Shake

1 1/2   ounces bourbon
1   ounce Jamaican dark rum
1   ounce heavy cream

Mix everything with cracked ice in shaker and strain into glass.

Jungle Juice

1   ounce Pisang Ambon
1/2   ounce gin
1/2   ounce apricot-flavored brandy
1/2   ounce lemon juice
        orange juice to fill glass

Mix everything with cracked ice in a shaker. Pour into a chilled old-fashioned glass. Add orange juice, Serve

KOSKELA

Kahlua Mudslide

1/2	ounce Coffee Liqueur
1	ounce heavy cream
1/2	ounce Irish Cream Liqueur
1/2	ounce vodka

Mix everything with cracked ice in a shaker. Strain into a chilled cocktail glass or put everything including cracked ice in a blender. Mix until frosty.

Kamikaze

1	ounce Triple Sec
1	ounce vodka
1	ounce lime juice

Mix everything with cracked ice in a shaker. Strain into a chilled cocktail glass.

Kona Cooler

1 1/2	ounces whiskey
3/4	ounce White Crème de Cacao
1	chunk pineapple
1	maraschino cherry

Mix everything except fruit with cracked ice in shaker and pour into glass. Garnish with fruit.

Lemonade Bomb Punch

1	can lemonade concentrate
3	cups vodka
8	cans beer

Mix the lemonade concentrate with the vodka instead of water in directions. Mix well and add the beer.

Long Island Iced Tea

1	ounce gin
1	ounce vodka
1	ounce light rum
1	ounce Triple Sec
2	ounces Sweet & Sour mix
	cola to fill glass

Add ice cubes to Collins glass. Add the alcohol and Sweet & Sour mix. Fill to top with cola. Add lemon twist for garnish.

Manhattan, The Original

1 1/2	ounces whiskey
1/4	ounce vermouth
	dash of Angostura Bitters
	maraschino cherry

Mix everything with plenty of ice in pitcher and strain into glass.

Manhattan, Perfect

1 1/2 ounces whiskey
1/2   ounce sweet vermouth
1/4   ounce dry vermouth
       dash of Angostura Bitters
       maraschino cherry

Mix all except cherry with cracked ice and strain into cocktail glass. Garnish with maraschino cherry.

Michelada

12	ounces beer
	juice of 1 lemon
2	dashes Worcestershire sauce
1	dash soy sauce
1	Tabasco® sauce
1	pinch black pepper
	salt to taste

Mix ingredients except beer in a Collins glass with lots of ice. Add beer at the end. Mix and enjoy.

Mimosa

| 6 | ounces Brut Champagne |
| 3 | ounces fresh orange juice |

Prechill champagne and orange juice. Mix together in wine goblet. Add ice if desired.

Monte Carlo

2	ounces rye whiskey
1/2	ounce Benedictine
2	dashes Angostura Bitters

Mix ingredients in shaker with ice. Strain into chilled cocktail glass.

Mint Julep

The mint julep originated in Williamsburg, Virginia in the seventeenth century. The art of mixing a fabulous authentic mint julep can make a julep go from mediocre to extraordinary. The perfect main ingredient in the julep is a 90 or 100 proof sour-mash Kentucky bourbon.

Steps to the perfect julep:

Break up 15-20 fresh mint leaves in the bottom of a silver or pewter tankard. Add a teaspoon of sugar and 2 tablespoons water. Muddle the leaves until they are well crushed and the sugar is dissolved. Fill tankard with finely crushed ice. Pour enough bourbon into tankard to come to an inch below the rim. After thoroughly stirring, add crushed ice to just below rim and float a teaspoon of Barbados rum on the top. Add 3-4 fresh mint sprigs on top for garnish. Enjoy!

Mojito

4	*fresh mint sprigs, plus 1 for garnish*
1	*tablespoon superfine sugar*
2	*tablespoons fresh lime juice*
3	*tablespoons white or gold rum*
2	*dashes bitters*
1/4	*cup club soda*

In a small bowl, crush the mint with the sugar until mint is coarsely chopped and sugar is light green. Add the lime juice, rum and bitters and stir to dissolve the sugar. Strain the mixture through a coarse sieve into a Collins glass filled with ice. Top with the soda and garnish with a mint sprig.

Old-Fashioned

2	ounces whiskey
1	cube sugar
1	orange slice
	dash of Angostura Bitters
	maraschino cherry
	lemon-lime soda (Sprite™ or 7-UP™) to fill glass

In an old-fashioned glass, muddle the sugar, bitters and orange slice. Add whiskey, stir. Add ice cubes and soda to fill glass. Garnish with a maraschino cherry.

Orange Blossom

1 1/2	ounce gin
1	ounce orange juice
	orange slice for garnish

Mix gin and orange juice with cracked ice in a shaker. Strain into a chilled cocktail glass. Garnish with orange slice.

Peaches and Cream

1	ounce Kahlua
1	ounce peach-flavored schnapps
2	ounces half & half

Mix everything with cracked ice in a shaker. Shake vigorously. Pour into a chilled Collins or highball glass.

Pink Lady

1 1/2   *ounces gin*
1   *ounce cream*
3   *ounces sour mix*
1/2   *teaspoon Grenadine*

Mix everything with cracked ice in a shaker. Shake vigorously. Strain into a chilled cocktail glass.

Rob Roy

1 1/2   *ounces scotch*
1/2   *ounce sweet vermouth*
        dash of Angostura Bitters
        maraschino cherry

Mix everything except cherry in shaker with ice. Strain into glass and garnish with cherry.

Rootbeer Float

1   *ounce rootbeer-flavored schnapps*
1   *ounce Kahlua*
        half & half

Mix schnapps and Kahlua in a shaker with ice. Pour into an old-fashioned glass. Fill with half & half.

Russian Coffee

1/2   *ounce vodka*
1 1/2 *ounces coffee-flavored liqueur (Kahlua)*
1   *ounce heavy cream*

Mix everything with cracked ice in shaker and pour into glass.

KOSKELA

Rusty Nail

1 1/2   ounces scotch
1   ounce Drambuie

Pour everything into glass with ice cubes and stir.

Sangria Punch

1   bottle good red wine (Cabernet Sauvignon)
1/2   cup sugar
1   cup orange juice
1   cup lemon juice
         whole cloves and cinnamon sticks

Mix all together except cloves and cinnamon sticks and chill in refrigerator for at least 12 hours. When ready to serve add the cloves and cinnamon sticks to taste.

Sangrita

1   ounce tequila
1   ounce Clamato juice
         few drops of hot pepper sauce
         dash of Worcestershire sauce

In one shot glass pour tequila. In another put other ingredients. Shoot with the tequila and chase with second shot.

Screw Driver

1 1/2   *ounces vodka*
4   *ounces orange juice*
         orange slice

Mix vodka and orange juice in a glass with several ice cubes. Garnish with orange slice.

Shamrock

1 1/2   *ounces Irish Whiskey*
1 1/2   *ounces Green Crème de Menthe*
2   *ounces heavy cream*
         maraschino cherry

Mix everything except cherry with cracked ice in shaker and pour into glass. Garnish with maraschino cherry.

Singapore Sling

2   *ounces gin*
1   *ounce cherry-flavored brandy*
         dash of Benedictine
         juice of 1/2 lemon
         club soda to fill glass
         lemon slice

Mix gin, brandy, benedictine, lemon juice and small amount of soda with some cracked ice in a shaker. Strain into a chilled Collins glass. Add more ice and fill with club soda. Garnish with lemon slice.

Slippery Nipple

1	ounce Sambuca
1/2	ounce vodka
1/2	ounce Irish Cream Liqueur

Put into a chilled cocktail glass in the order given.

Smith and Kearns

1	ounce Kahlua
1	ounce light cream
	carbonated water

Pour Kahlua and cream into a highball glass filled with ice and stir well. Fill with carbonated water, stir and serve.

Stinger

| 1 1/2 | ounces brandy |
| 1/2 | ounce White Crème de Menthe |

Mix ingredients in shaker with cracked ice. Strain into a cocktail glass.

Strawberry Margarita

1 1/2 ounces tequila
1/2 ounce Triple Sec
1/2 ounce strawberry-flavored liqueur or schnapps
1 ounce lime juice
fresh or frozen strawberries as garnish

Salt-rim a chilled cocktail or margarita glass by rubbing the rim with lime and dipping into salt. Combine all ingredients except garnish and 1-2 ounces cracked ice in a blender. Mix well and pour into cocktail glass. Garnish with strawberry.

Tequila Iced Coffee

1 1/2 ounces tequila
1 teaspoon sugar
1/2 teaspoon lime or lemon juice
strong black coffee to fill

Fill a highball glass 2/3 full of ice. Add above ingredients and stir well.

Tequila Sunrise

1 1/2 ounces tequila
3 ounces orange juice
3/4 ounce Grenadine
juice of 1/2 lime
slice of lime

Mix all ingredients except grenadine and lime slice in shaker with ice. Pour into a Collins glass. Add additional ice if desired. Slowly pour in Grenadine and do not stir. Garnish with lime slice.

Tom Collins

2 1/2   *ounces gin*
1 1/2   *ounces lemon juice*
1/2   *ounce sugar syrup*
         maraschino cherry
         club soda to fill

Mix everything except cherry and soda in a Collins glass filled 2/3 full of cracked ice. Fill with soda. Garnish with the maraschino cherry.

Tornado

1   *ounce whiskey*
2   *ounces rum*
1   *ounce vodka*
2   *ounces Coca-Cola™*
1/2   *tablespoon sugar*

Mix everything except sugar, ice and Coca-Cola™. Stir well. Stir in sugar and cola. Pour over highball glass filled 2/3 full of ice.

Tropical Splendor

6	ounces Tropical Passion soda
2	ounces rum

Pour rum in Collins glass filled with cracked ice. Add soda to fill.

Vanilla Coke

1	ounce vanilla-flavored vodka
3	ounces Coca-Cola ™

Fill tall glass with ice and pour over the above ingredients.

Vodka Cooler

1 1/2	ounces vodka
1/2	ounce sweet vermouth
1/2	ounce lemon juice
1/2	ounce sugar syrup
	club soda to fill

Mix everything except soda in a shaker with cracked ice. Pour into Collins glass. Fill with club soda.

Whiskey Sour

2   ounces blended whiskey
       juice of 1/2 lemon
1/2   teaspoon powdered sugar
1/2   slice lemon
       maraschino cherry

Mix all ingredients except lemon slice and cherry in a shake with cracked ice. Strain into an old-fashioned glass. Garnish with lemon slice and cherry.

White Russian

1 1/2 ounces vodka
1   ounce White Crème de Cacao
3/4   ounce heavy cream

Mix everything with cracked ice in shaker and strain into cocktail glass.

Zanzibar

1 1/2 ounces dry vermouth
1/4   ounce lemon juice
1/2   ounce gin
1/4   teaspoon sugar

Mix ingredients in shaker with ice. Strain into a cocktail glass. Garnish with twist of lemon.

The late Trader Vic (Victor Bergeron) was the inventor of many new and exciting drinks. He changed the drinking habits of many Americans when he owned the Don the Beachcomber of Hollywood. Here he would make exotic Polynesian-style rum drinks that became the rage in the 1940's and '50's. Some of his famous drink concoctions include the Fog Cutter, Mai Tai, and Scorpion.

Fog Cutter

1 1/2	ounces light rum
1/2	ounce gin
1/2	ounce brandy
1	ounce orange juice
3	tablespoons lemon juice
1 1/2	teaspoons Orgeat Syrup

Shake all ingredients in a shaker and strain into a tall Collins glass over ice cubes. Top with a teaspoon of sweet sherry and serve.

Mai Tai

1	ounce light rum
1	ounce dark rum
1/2	ounce Curaçao
1/4	ounce sugar syrup
1/4	ounce Orgeat Syrup
	lime peel, mint sprig, pineapple stick

Mix all ingredients except lime peel, mint, and pineapple with cracked ice in a shaker. Pour into a double old-fashioned glass and garnish with lime peel, mint and pineapple stick. This is the original Trader Vic's recipe.

Scorpion

2   *ounces light rum*
1   *ounce brandy*
1/2   *ounce Orgeat Syrup*
2   *ounces orange juice*
1 1/2 *ounces lemon juice*
2   *dashes sugar syrup*
        gardenia

Mix all ingredients except flower in a blender with shaved ice. Pour into a chilled white wine glass and garnish with the gardenia. This is an authentic Trader Vic's recipe.

KOSKELA

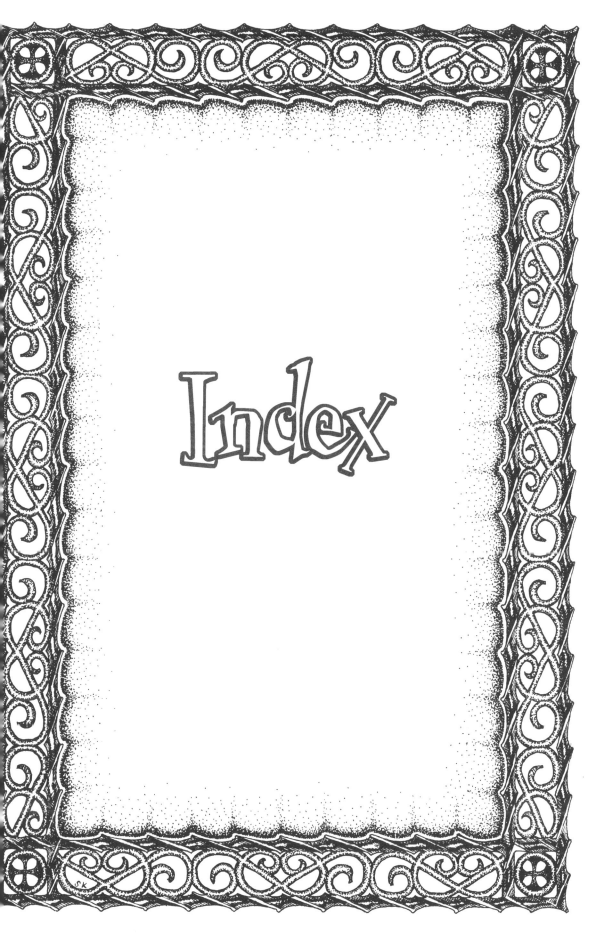

Index

A

B

C

D

F

G

H

I

J

Index

67

ORDER FORM

If you would like to order additional copies of this book or sample some of our other fine products, please fill out the form below and mail to:

YOUR POINT OF PURCHASE RETAILER
OR
R.A.L. ENTERPRISES
Suite 136, 5000 A. West Esplanade Avenue, Metairie, Louisiana 70006

TITLE		COST	QUANTITY	TOTAL
The New Orleans Bartender	80 pages	$7.95	_____	_____
New Orleans - French Quarter	32 pages	$4.95	_____	_____
Basic and Easy New Orleans Cooking	64 pages	$7.95	_____	_____
Favorite Recipes from New Orleans	64 pages	$7.95	_____	_____
Plantation Country Guide	64 pages	$7.95	_____	_____
Cookin' In High Cotton	64 pages	$7.95	_____	_____
Cookin' New Orleans Style	64 pages	$7.95	_____	_____
Cookin' Country Cajun (Soft Cover)	64 pages	$7.95	_____	_____
Cookin' on the Mississippi (Hard Cover)	64 pages	$8.95	_____	_____
Cookin' on the Mississippi (Soft Cover)	64 pages	$7.95	_____	_____
Historic Houses of the Deep South	64 pages	$12.95	_____	_____
New Orleans	64 pages	$8.95	_____	_____
Laminated New Orleans Placemats	Set of 4	$9.95	_____	_____
Laminated Louisiana Plantation Placemats	Set of 4	$9.95	_____	_____
Laminated Mississippi Plantation Placemats	Set of 4	$9.95	_____	_____
Louisiana/Mississippi Coloring Book	32 pages	$4.95	_____	_____
Recipe Box Cards	Set of 10	$5.95	_____	_____
New Orleans Notes & Stationery	64 Piece Set	$9.95	_____	_____

Postage & Handling $2.50 _____

TOTAL _____

❏ Check Enclosed ❏ Visa ❏ MasterCard ❏ American Express ❏ Discover

Card Number _____ Expiration Date _____

Name _____

Address _____

City _____ State _____ Zip _____

Daytime Phone (_____) _____

All items are satisfaction guaranteed and your purchase price will be promptly refunded if returned within 30 days.
Please allow two to four weeks for delivery. No foreign orders please.